Remember Rudy

Tess Padmore

Illustrations by Stephen Scherer

The Old Souls Café Publishing
www.wolfclanllc.com/rememberrudy

Text copyright 2019 by Tess Padmore

All rights reserved. This book or parts thereof may not be reproduced in any form, stored in any retrieval system, or transmitted in any form by any means—electronic, mechanical, photocopy, recording, or otherwise—without written permission of the publisher, except as provided by the United States copyright law.

Illustrations by Stephen Scherer

ISBN 978-0-9998710-0-3

First Printing, 2019

The Old Souls Café Publishing
1115 E. Main St., Box 46
Rochester, NY 14609
www.wolfclanllc.com/rememberrudy

Dedication

To Sandy Ryan from *Around the Bend*,
for breeding the best dog ever.

Remember when...

we brought you home, and
Athena carried you like a baby?

You'd unravel toilet tissue
and prance from room to room
with a long ribbon behind you.

It took weeks to convince
you I was the alpha dog.

You met Dr. Brownstein
for the first time, and she asked
why you put both paws on
her while she held you up.

I told her you wanted a hug, and from that day on she called you Rudy, Rudy, Patootie.

Remember how you'd come
to me whenever I cried and insist
that I let you lie beside me?

Lewis would use you as a two pound weight and do arm lifts.

Athena scared you
with laundry baskets,

and vacuum cleaners.

Remember how
Athena would sneak food
to you under the table?

You'd crawl under the covers and sleep all night with Athena.

You'd roll on your back,
bare your tiny teeth,
and laugh that funny
little laugh.

You'd show Lewis
my potato chip hiding places,
so he'd share with you.

We all played hide and seek.

Remember when you figured out that ice came from the refrigerator door and would come running whenever someone tried to fill a glass?

You decided to get your own ice, and we watched you jump until you hit the mark and got your own ice chips.

You figured out that doorknobs open doors, and you worked so hard to open the back door but never could.

You'd back up and sneeze repeatedly when you wanted something.

Whenever I spoke on the phone
you would sit patiently, waiting to see
if it was my mother, "Mommy."

When I put the phone next your head
you would tilt it to the side,
point your ears up and move
your eyes from side to side.

You shocked us all one day when you spoke into the phone to her, saying "hewwo."

Remember when you'd lie on my stomach and we would wrestle on the living room floor?

I'd tickle you and you'd laugh and laugh.

You'd sit next to me on the steps with our butts on the same step and our legs down on the next step.

Sitting next to you on the steps,
I'd ask if you wanted to snuzzle
and you'd go behind me,
put a front paw on each shoulder,
and lick me behind the ear.

You would run up behind me
on the steps and pull my ponytail
until I got up to play with you.

Remember when Earlene
didn't believe that you went to bed
every night at 8 o'clock...
until she came to visit?

Every time Earlene visited
the house, you'd push
the bathroom door open with
your nose, then walk away.

She'd stand there naked, screaming.

You escaped two times,
running as fast as you could.
We thought we were going
to lose you . . .

until you heard Athena's cry, and you ran back just as fast to see about her.

Remember when you
escaped the last time?

Moving at a slow trot you
made it around the corner,
and I, with my now arthritic knees,
could only manage a semi-fast
limp to try and catch you.

The ice storm knocked out the heat, and I dressed you and wrapped you in a blanket against my body to keep you warm.

We had a severe rainstorm
one March, and you got loose
in the back yard late at night.

You rolled and rolled in
the mud underneath the
weeping willow tree.

You made me chase
you around and around
until I was covered in mud.

I finally gave up after a
half hour and eventually coaxed
you into the house.

You looked like you had
"gone to ground."

We were both covered
in mud, and I had to
give you a full bath.

You'd grab the bubble wrap from every package, bare your tiny front teeth, and pop each bubble individually.

I came home from a
full month in the hospital,
and we sat on those same
steps. I was crying
and you were whining
and peeing.

You lay at my feet and
didn't let anyone come
near me until I was healed.

Najir was born, and you couldn't figure out what he was—only that very smelly stuff came out of him.

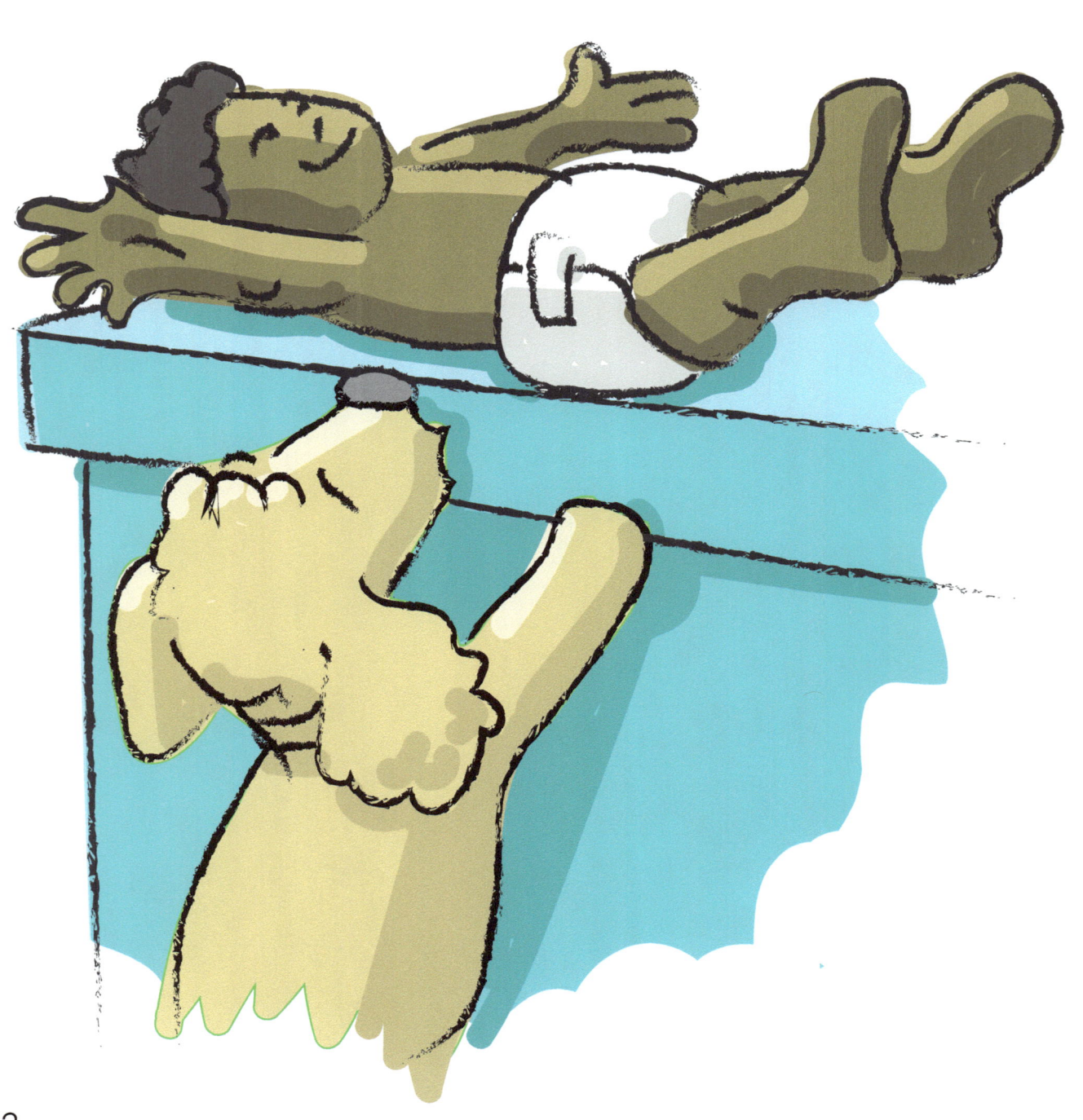

Najir would come to visit,
and you would swallow his socks
when they hit the floor.

Najir would tell his friends you were his dog with such pride.

He told me he was old enough to walk you by himself.

You held your head high
even though, at 15, you were
getting to be old for a dog.

And then the time came. I took you to my bed, held you in my arms and let you sleep because I knew it was our last day together.

I held your face in my hands and spoke to you until you found peace.

Rest in Peace,
Rudy Padmore.

7/5/95 –11/17/10

www.ingramcontent.com/pod-product-compliance
Lightning Source LLC
Chambersburg PA
CBHW060822090426
42738CB00002B/71